CREATE YOUR OWN *Dream* FEATHERS

Peggy Holt

American Quilter's Society
P. O. Box 3290 • Paducah, KY 42002-3290
www.AmericanQuilter.com

Located in Paducah, Kentucky, the American Quilter's Society (AQS) is dedicated to promoting the accomplishments of today's quilters. Through its publications and events, AQS strives to honor today's quiltmakers and their work and to inspire future creativity and innovation in quiltmaking.

Executive Book Editor: Andi Milam Reynolds
Senior Editor: Linda Baxter Lasco
Copy Editor: Barbara Pitman
Graphic Design: Lynda Smith
Cover Design: Michael Buckingham
Quilt Photography: Charles R. Lynch

All rights reserved. No part of this book may be reproduced, stored in any retrieval system, or transmitted in any form, or by any means including but not limited to electronic, mechanical, photocopy, recording or otherwise, without the written consent of the author and publisher. Patterns may be copied for personal use only, including the right to enter contests; quilter should seek written permission from the author and pattern designer before entering. Credit must be given to the author, pattern designer, and publisher on the quilt label and contest entry form. Written permission from author, pattern designer, and publisher must be sought to raffle or auction quilts made from this book. While every effort has been made to ensure that the contents of this publication are as accurate and correct as possible, no warranty is provided nor results guaranteed. Since the author and AQS have no control over individual skills or choice of materials and tools, they do not assume responsibility for the use of this information.

Attention Photocopying Service: Please note the following—publisher and author give permission to photocopy pages 68–94 for personal use only.

Additional copies of this book may be ordered from the American Quilter's Society, PO Box 3290, Paducah, KY 42002-3290, or online at www.AmericanQuilter.com.

Text ©2012, Author, Peggy Holt
Artwork ©2012, American Quilter's Society

Library of Congress Cataloging-in-Publication Data

Holt, Peggy, 1946-
  Create your own dream feathers / by Peggy Holt.
    p. cm.
  Summary: "Continuous line designs to create quilting patterns-feathers, butterflies, hearts, paisleys, and more. Three concepts underlie this approach to free-motion quilting. Designs work for longarm, midarm, or domestic quilting, and hand quilting"-- Provided by publisher.
  Includes bibliographical references and index.
  ISBN 978-1-60460-020-9 (alk. paper)
  1. Quilting--Patterns. I. Title.
  TT835.H556235 2012
  746.46--dc23
                        2011044726

Thank You!

John Donne wrote "…no man is an island," implying that we all depend upon one another. The same may be said of quilters. The sum total of our knowledge is the accumulation of all we have read, observed, and practiced. We learn from the mistakes and successes of those who came before us. We surround ourselves with those who will support and encourage us.

This book would not have come to fruition if it weren't for a number of people who kept me on task and on track.

I am so thankful for those who were instrumental in the revival of quilting in the early seventies. They opened doors and paved the way for so many of us who were ready for a new avenue of creative expression.

Thank you to the editorial staff at American Quilter's Society who were willing to take a risk on an unknown author; your confidence in me is humbling. Special thanks to Andi Reynolds and Linda Lasco for their encouragement and advice.

Many thanks to my friends for allowing their quilts to be included in the book: Chris Milodragovich, Marguerite Shattuck, Pat Cross, and Robin Hall. It is a joy to be able to share your pieces. I particularly thank Myrna Nyberg for sharing her amazing gift of appliqué.

I want to thank my family for their support: To my son, Jason, who grew up with an appreciation for fabric and cluttered sewing rooms, and who knows the difference between "fabrics" and "materials;" to his wife, Sierra, who is raising my grandchildren, Zora and Linden, to love and honor what Grandma does. And especially, I thank my husband, Bill, my companion and friend for over forty years; without you I would have fallen and never bothered to get up. Thank you for giving me the gift of time and the joy of your support.

I thank God for those He has placed in my life. And I am eternally grateful to Him for the gift of an appreciation for this lovely art form: The Quilt.

Title page: APPLIQUÉ SAMPLER, *detail. Full quilt on page 55.*

Table of Contents

Introduction

Oh no, not another book about feathers! Well, yes, it is, actually. But unlike many others, this book will let your creative spirit soar, allowing you to create original, beautiful designs, unique to you and unique to each quilt.

To be sure, feathers are not new to the quilting world; they grace many a vintage quilt. Nor, for that matter are spineless feathers unique. They are the natural result of finding ways to create continuous line quilting for those of us who machine quilt. The concept of using the feather in a new and unique way is what makes this book different from many available on the market today.

Dream Feathers! It all began with a dream. I have particularly admired borders of feathers as they undulate up and down creating hills and valleys. My experimentation had led me to creating spineless feathers. These spineless feathers are versatile, molding to unusual spaces and all-over meandering. The dream melded these two con-

cepts and when I awoke I knew I had something a little different. Some quick sketches confirmed my suspicion and Peggy's Dream Feathers were born.

Here you will find simplified directions for creating beautiful Standard Feathers as well as Peggy's Dream Feathers. You will learn how to manipulate shapes and how to embellish them. In addition, you will be armed with a new concept of how to unify your quilting choices to impart a sense of fluidity and grace to your quilts. There is something disturbing about a quilt that has been quilted with a hodge podge of shapes and motifs. My method will help you look at the quilt as a whole, giving beautiful results.

I am a longarm quilter and the book has been written from that perspective. Most designs are continuous-line or have a minimum of starts and stops. However, all of the designs can be executed on a domestic machine or even by hand. And the designing concepts are certainly universal for all disciplines.

General Instructions

How to Use this Book

The book presents three distinct concepts: Learning to draw a pleasing Standard Feather, learning the Dream Feather, and using Base Shapes to help unify your quilting designs. It is intended to help the beginner analyze and study how a feather is created and to inspire the advanced quilter to develop new and original designs.

If you are new to using feathers in your quilting, you will want to read the chapter on Graceful Feathers (pages 9–11). You will learn to analyze your feathers to see how they can be improved.

Those of you who are more advanced could probably skip directly to the chapter on The Dream Feather (pages 12–13). Of course, you run the risk of missing some fantastic little hint that you may not have thought of before, but you can always go back and read the earlier chapter another time.

Once you are comfortable with feathers in general, you are introduced to Peggy's Dream Feathers. These feathers are spineless and rely upon themselves for form. They float on air in beauty and elegance.

Finally, there are the Base Shapes. I found that I was using these shapes repeatedly throughout a quilt. They provide continuity and cohesiveness to a quilt.

Scattered throughout the book you will find suggestions for exercises. These are paper and pencil suggestions that will help you familiarize yourself with various concepts. Once again your sketch pads or newsprint will come in handy. If you do the exercises in a journal, you will have quick and easy access for future reference.

The Base Shape Concept

The Glossary of Shapes (pages 67–75) contains all the shapes referred to throughout the book. You choose a Base Shape, manipulate it to suit your quilt, then embellish it with feathers or other motifs.

Too often we see quilts that have a variety of designs— feathers here, flowers there, a few leaves stuck somewhere else. The quilt looks like a sampler of quilting motifs. By repeating one shape throughout the quilt you will develop a beautiful, unified design for the entire quilt.

A single Base Shape can be used as a stand-alone design in a block; it can be used as a swag; it can be embellished with feathers or leaves or curls. The original shape can be manipulated to make it fatter or skinnier; it can be mirrored. Individual motifs can be set side-by-side in a border or one can serve as a perfect centerpiece in a border with garlands of feathers flowing outward to the edges of a quilt. Set off shapes with crosshatching, piano keys, or chevrons. Use them for trapunto.

Oh my, the possibilities are endless and mind-boggling! Where will this unique concept lead you?

Tools to Have on Hand

To make the best use of this book you will need a few basic tools. To be sure, you can peruse the book without drawing any of the ideas, but if you are like me, you will soon be scrambling to find a pencil and some paper, so you might as well gather the tools together before you settle into your easy chair with that cup of tea.

Newsprint—Lots of Newsprint!

I purchase newspaper end rolls from the local newspaper. They are cheap and plentiful. I use them to draw full-sized patterns and to trace motifs. Having this inexpensive paper around allows me to draw in a large scale and get a good feel of how a motif is going to perform on a quilt. Newsprint is also great for making initial patterns.

If you do not have access to end rolls, large pads of newsprint work. These are usually found wherever art supplies are sold such as craft and variety stores. You can also buy boxes of newsprint sheets from moving companies.

Template Plastic

I suggest that you trace at least the Base Shapes (pages 68–75) onto template plastic. Make several different sizes. Place these shapes in a manila envelope and tape the envelope into the back of this book. In addition, you will probably come up with more ideas for Base Shapes. Make templates of those as well.

Miscellaneous Supplies

Rulers and straight-edges
Mechanical pencils
Erasers
Journals or sketch pads
Clear vinyl
Marking tools
Manila envelope

Tips and Hints

Markers

My preference for marking is white school chalk. It usually brushes off easily. Use a microfiber cloth as an eraser. Any residue can be removed with a spritz of water or will come out when the quilt is laundered.

An unexpected tool for removing chalk marks is a rubber kitchen glove. Just slip it on and gently rub back and forth with the grain of the fabric. A rubber gripper used to loosen jar lids works as well. Caution: Brightly colored gloves or grippers may transfer color to your quilt. The residue may brush off easily, but why take a chance?

Clear Vinyl

Clear vinyl is a great tool for auditioning designs before actually stitching. Any weight of vinyl will work; it just needs to be clear. You can purchase vinyl in the home dec or upholstery department of many fabric and craft stores. It is also found in many home improvement and hardware stores.

You also need low tack painter's tape and a dry erase pen.

Cut a piece of vinyl 1"–2" larger than the area where you want to work. For instance, if you are designing for a 12" block, then cut the vinyl at least 14". Tape all edges of the vinyl with painter's tape. This will provide a visual stopping point. It is very easy to draw right off the vinyl, so do not skip this step; you will regret it at some point if you don't use the tape!

Lay the vinyl over the area you want to work with and use a dry erase marker to draw your design. You can instantly see if you like the motif. Making changes is easy. Simply erase and try again.

Note: If you don't erase the lines, they may become permanent over time, or they may leave shadows on the vinyl. So if you want to re-use the vinyl, be sure to erase the designs once you have made a pattern from them.

From Pattern to Quilt

Although there are several ways to transfer a design from a vinyl practice sheet to a quilt, I am most likely to simply use the drawing as a reference and stitch freehand.

My next choice would be to chalk in the design for a little more control. I use regular school chalk. Keep a sharp point by using a small pencil sharpener.

Other Methods

There are other methods for transferring a design onto a quilt top including making a stencil or stitching through tear-away paper. Of course, you could also trace directly onto the quilt top before loading the quilt onto your machine or layering the quilt sandwich.

Using construction lines as boundaries also works for spacing individual designs. When quilting a single block, all you have to do is situate the Base Shape within the block, then feather along the shape, filling the space to the outer seam of the block.

I have also used the laser on my longarm machine to follow a drawn design. Place the pattern on your table and align as you would for a pantograph or lay the pattern to the side directly on the quilt and position the laser for stitching.

Sometimes, I get so involved in watching feathers magically appear on a quilt that I flow right into a space where another motif should be! To prevent this accidental encroachment, I chalk in general boundary lines; I know that I cannot feather beyond that line.

I used boundary lines with REMEMBERING: BELLE'S STAR (page 65). I knew that I wanted a curl of feathers around each star, emanating from the large star. However, the space between the stars was limited, so I chalked in a guideline that separated the two areas and then feathered to my heart's content within the boundaries I had created.

Below are two photos showing the result of this process.

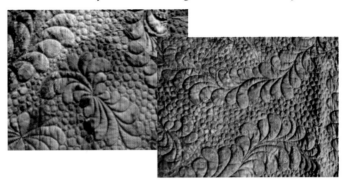

The feathers surrounding the stars are on either side. I chalked in general guidelines for both sets of feathers. Floating motifs fill odd spaces, and pebbling fills in the background.

Keeping a Journal

A journal is an essential tool for me. It can be as simple as a cheap school notepad or any of the myriad of journals and sketchpads available today.

Although it is not an absolute necessity, I strongly recommend that you keep some kind of a journal. My journal of choice is an artist's sketch pad. I recommend one large enough to allow development of a design. The journal allows you to sketch out ideas and have a permanent reminder of all the beautiful ideas you have developed. It also allows you to keep a record of your own personal development.

Don't worry about the "beauty" of the journal. This is for your private use and not for public viewing unless you choose to share it. Many of the designs in this book are renderings of my original sketches. Although they are not necessarily lovely at the doodling stage, many have become the basis for some pretty designs.

I also have lined notebooks everywhere...by the phone, in the bedroom, at the computer, in the car, or anywhere else that I feel is necessary. I never know when the muse will strike, providing inspiration by a line or a curve that just begs to be feathered.

In my journal I draw one motif over and over again, playing with sizes and shapes, curls, and flourishes to see what will happen. It is amazing how a simple shape can undergo so many transformations.

I date my doodling just to document my progress. In addition I will note the source of the inspiration. It might be a dream, or a floor tile; sometimes it's something I've seen in a magazine; sometimes it is just the result of letting my mind wander.

I cannot emphasize enough how important it is to doodle and draw. This is what imprints the designs in your brain and allows you to make them your own.

Once I get a design I like, I pull out the newsprint and draw it full-sized, over and over. I particularly like newsprint for this process. A small page does not allow the full body movement you need, especially when quilting with the longarm machine. This is when I decide if more detail needs to be added to balance the density of the feathers. It is when I determine if the design really will work.

Some people like to use dry erase boards for doodling, and they certainly have their place. However, at some point you have to erase the board to make room for more doodling. Then you run the risk of losing some wonderful designs that may just be the spark of a brand new, beautiful motif. If your doodling is on paper you have the option of keeping it if it is spec-

tacular, or tossing it if you really never want to be reminded of it ever again.

The Quilt Whisperer

I am often asked how I come up with ideas for quilting. I must admit that sometimes I wonder the same thing! Since developing the concept of Base Shapes, I have found it easier to create a cohesive plan for quilting.

Still, my modus operandi continues to be the same. I begin by studying the basic lines and shapes in the quilt. I look for secondary designs created by color or I look for cues in the fabrics themselves. And I physically feel the quilt. I run my hands over and over the various spaces, familiarizing myself with the "feel." I refer to myself as "The Quilt Whisperer." I truly let the color, texture, and small nuances of the piecing enter my senses through touch. I feel the flow of the quilt teaching my brain to respond.

It sounds a bit mystic, I suppose, but once I get that "feel" ingrained in my mind, I usually get more than one idea that will work on the quilt. The difficulty then becomes one of making a choice!

I very rarely plan out every section of a quilt, and I almost never mark the top before I load it on the machine. It works for me, but it might not work for you. Still, I trust my instincts and the gifts God gave me.

So, are you ready? Let's learn about Feathers and Base Shapes, Butterflies and Hearts, and more. Oh my!

Graceful Feathers

All feathers begin with a basic shape. It is how we embellish, enhance, and develop it that makes these beautiful motifs come alive.

We will start with that shape, add it to a vein, or build it onto itself. Then we will experiment with other shapes that the feather can enhance.

Anatomy of a Feather

Let's take a look at how a Standard Feather is formed.

Basically it is a paisley shape. It is a closed unit that can stand alone or it can be attached to a spine.

Feather paisley shape

Some people look at feathers as half a heart. Although this is a good place to start, you can see by the illustration that is not exactly true. The half heart stops at the spine while a true feather, the paisley shape, is independent of the spine. The half heart depends on the spine to close it while the paisley can stand alone.

Half heart

A good way to get started learning the feel of feathers is to draw them as free-standing units.

Exercise

Fill a sheet of paper with these paisley shapes. Draw them in all directions and in all sizes. Don't worry about their beauty right now, just draw them over and over.

As you draw, analyze what you are doing when you get feathers that actually please you. Here is what you will probably find.

Well-formed, beautiful feathers have two major components that make them beautiful. The tip of the feather would create a circle if you were to continue the line. This is shown with a dotted line in the illustration below. I admit that I don't always accomplish this perfect circle. Still, it is the goal.

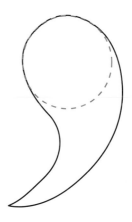

The feather closes completely. It does not require a spine. This is why the half heart doesn't work to create the beautiful, graceful lines that we are looking for in a feather; it requires a spine to be complete.

Note the red circled areas in the following illustrations. With a well-formed feather, the line tends to curve back toward its origination point. With the half heart, the line ends at the spine.

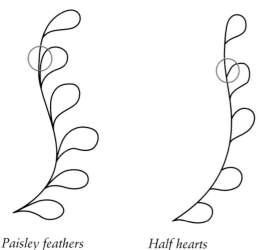

Paisley feathers   *Half hearts*

Additionally, when the feathers are lined up opposite each other, they will still maintain their integrity as a feather or paisley. They create elegant, flowing curves and are independent of a spine. Two half hearts will create—well, they create a heart! The beauty of a feather is lost.

Paisley feathers   *Half hearts*

Important! No matter how long and curved or short and stubby you make each feather, it will always resemble a paisley shape; it will have the circular shape at the top, and it will be completely closed, independent of a spine. Experiment with different shapes and sizes, keeping these principles in mind.

Continue to draw the individual feathers until you feel comfortable and happy with them. There are plastic templates available for these feathers, and you may want to check them out, but the sooner you get used to drawing them freehand, the sooner you will be able to stitch feathers without having to mark your quilts first.

You will soon be drawing these paisley shapes on everything—your grocery list, scraps of paper, envelopes, the newspaper, napkins, even the church bulletin. Nothing is safe from doodling once you get the addiction.

Exercise
Now it's time to try these beautiful shapes on a spine.

To begin, draw a long graceful curve. Starting at the bottom of the curved line, draw one feather on the spine. Use the spine as a guide.

Draw feathers individually to start with. We will eventually nestle them together, but for now just draw them onto the spine. Strive for a graceful look. If you are very, very new to feathers, don't worry about continuous motion right now. Referring to the two illustrations (above left), note how a well-formed feather returns to its origination point, whereas the half heart ends on the spine. Strive to get the return more or less parallel to or on top of the spine as opposed to having it just meet the spine. It's all a matter of angle in relation to the spine.

After you have been playing with feathers for a while you will automatically start backtracking along the spine as you move from one feather to the next.

The easiest way for most people to make feathers is from the bottom up on a vertical spine. Start there, but graduate to feathering spines in other directions. Try them from the top down, side to side, left to right, and right to left.

As you practice you will notice that your feathers are becoming closer and closer together and more uniform. You will probably also realize that you have quit making each feather individually, and that you are automatically following up the spine with your pencil to get to the next feather.

Spineless Feathers

So now you are ready to nestle the feathers together without a drawn spine. When feathers are nestled together it is necessary to backtrack along previous stitching.

Exercise

Begin by drawing a single paisley shape. You now have two different ways of backtracking. You can backtrack along the length as indicated by the red arrows.

Start

Backtracking along the length

This method is commonly referred to as the Longarm Feather. When stitched this way, you often see the feathers slightly separated. This less formal method is perfectly acceptable and does not detract from their beauty. In fact, these are quite beautiful in their own right.

Alternatively, you can backtrack along the tip. This method produces formal, elegant feathers.

Start

Backtracking along the tip

Most illustrations in this book are done in this more formal technique, but you certainly can do them less formally as well. And as we will see, they can even be combined with other embellishments.

Both ways work and each has its own look and feel to it. Neither is wrong, and doing it one way does not preclude doing it the other way another time. It is just a matter of what look you wish to achieve.

The Dream Feather

A Dream Feather builds upon itself or another shape and is independent of a spine.

Now that you have the basics of Standard Feather making, let's move on to the Dream Feather. One of the beauties of the Dream Feather is that it suits wide exterior borders as well as narrow bands within the quilt with no measuring or fuss.

There is nothing more beautiful and elegant than a border filled with feathers gracefully flowing on an undulating vine. Traditionally this effect is the result of careful measuring and considerable marking of the quilt. There is most certainly a place for these techniques and Dream Feathers do not necessarily replace them. Dream Feathers are just another way to achieve this effect. They will be slightly less than perfectly formal, but still have great elegance.

Exercise

Sometimes it is less confusing to read through all directions first, but I would suggest that you just plunge in and take one step at a time with this exercise. Since Dream Feathers originated as a border motif, we will begin there.

Draw two parallel lines on newsprint. They can be at any width, but make them at least 4" apart for ease. This represents your border.

Lightly sketch in a third horizontal line to delineate the middle of your "border;" sketch in a vertical line to indicate the center. Add vertical lines to both ends to represent the ends of the border. Make this "border" at least 20" long.

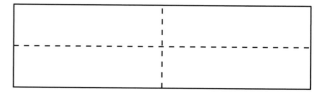

Draw 2 Pumpkin Seed Base Shapes at the vertical center line. You can use any of the Pumpkin Seed Base Shapes found in the Glossary (page 70) or draw them freehand.

Draw in your first four feathers, following the arrows. You will backtrack on the tips as explained in the previous chapter (page 11). The four feathers create a graceful shell. Keep these points in mind: The tip of every feather touches the bottom line of the border; each feather heads back to the original starting point.

The length of the fourth feather should come well above your horizontal center line. This is the secret to creating the Dream Feather. The farther over that center line the fourth feather is, the more curve you will achieve.

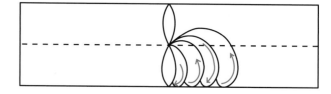

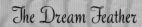

The return stroke of the fourth feather creates a base for the upper shell of feathers.

Now begin the upper shell by tucking the first feather against the upper Pumpkin Seed. This time you will make more feathers.

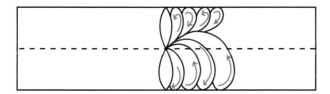

Continue making feathers until you have once again gone beyond the horizontal center mark and created another shell set. Once you have done so, begin working feathers on the bottom again. It bears repeating: Going well over the center horizontal line creates the desired variation in the size of the individual feathers.

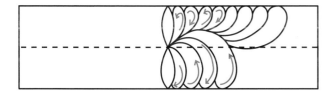

Alternate feathers above and below the center horizontal line to the end of the border. The final set of feathers should conform to the ends of your border. It may end with the upper feathers or the lower feathers.

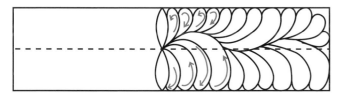

Repeat on the other side to complete the design. It is best if you can end with the same treatment at both ends of the border. This will produce the most formal effect, but if they're not the same, it is still a lovely design.

Things to remember when making Dream Feathers:

The tips of all feathers generally extend to the top and bottom lines of the border.

The final feather in each shell set must go beyond the horizontal midpoint.

Using a template to establish the Base Shape center will ensure continuity. The viewer's eye will be drawn to the consistency of the Base Shape.

Use the same number of feathers on either side of the center shape. Try to bring the final feather of the first shell above the horizon equally on both the left and right sides. After these first feathers are created, the viewer will not be aware if there are fewer or more feathers, or if there are slight variations. This is the beauty of hand-guided quilting.

Now that you understand the basics for the Dream Feather, it is time to apply the concept to the Base Shapes.

Base Shapes & the Dream Feather

The Base Shapes (pages 68–75) are used as the foundation for Standard Feathers or Dream Feathers, as well as for other curls, furls, and flourishes. Standard Feathers use the line of the Base Shape as a spine. Dream Feathers begin with the Base Shape, but subsequent feathers build upon previous feathers and are independent of the Base Shape.

Playing with Paisleys

A good place to begin is with the original Paisley Shape. Now this basic shape becomes a Base Shape. Let's feather a feather!

Draw a Paisley Base Shape freehand or use the shape in the Glossary (page 68).

Feather up the right side with Standard Feathers, using the side of the Base Shape as a guide. Your feathers can be tight and uniform or long and elegant. Remember, neither is wrong; each has its place.

Tight and uniform feathers

Long and elegant feathers

You might combine the tight feathers with the longer more flowing feathers as shown here.

Combining feathers

Try other variations. Maybe your space will call for flowing feathers on both sides of the Base Shape.

Or perhaps you need to add more at the bottom providing an anchor for the design.

The three previous illustrations all employ the Paisley Base Shape and Standard Feathers.

Now try the Dream Feather on a Paisley Base Shape. This motif starts out the same as the previous designs but instead of using the side of the original Base Shape as a spine, bring the feathers farther out and return them more in the direction of the original starting point. Remember, each feather will reach out to a common horizontal plane, indicated by the drawn line in the figure.

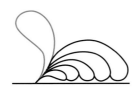

If you are having trouble aligning the feathers, lightly mark a line using chalk. Eventually, this will become automatic for you. This could also be a seam line on an actual quilt.

Once you have a nice long line to work with, start making the upper feathers. Tuck the first feather up against the Paisley Base Shape and continue outward along the length of the previous feather. Follow the directional arrows in the figure.

How you finish this off depends entirely on your whim and the space available for the motif. The feathers are numbered in the illustration below to help you identify the sequence.

Start

There is no right or wrong way to do this. It is purely a matter of what pleases you and what space you need to fill. Here is a Paisley Base Shape that is embellished with the Standard Feather and the Dream Feather combined.

The design starts with the Paisley Base Shape with Standard Feathers along the entire length of one side. The long side of the last feather is used as a base for the next set of feathers, taking them away from the original Paisley Base Shape, thus creating Dream Feathers.

Once you start playing with the Paisley Base Shape, you will see how truly endless this can be. No piece of paper will be safe when the muse hits. You will be drawing these on everything.

Is your head swimming yet? Well, hang on, because the fun has just begun!

So far we have been experimenting with the Paisley Base Shape. We have used the shape as a base for adding Standard Feathers or Dream Feathers. The same concept works for the other Base Shapes as well.

Here are some designs to get you started. These may look complicated but they all start with a Base Shape and are embellished with the Standard Feathers, Dream Feathers, or both. The sky is the limit!

Triple Paisley Base Shapes

The Triple Paisley Base Shape (page 69) works best when the Base Shape is larger than the Dream Feathers.

The addition of longer, narrower feathers provides the contrast to the larger Base Shape.

Exercise

Draw a Triple Paisley Base Shape freehand or use the shape in the glossary (page 69) and play with some possibilities. Below are two examples. Note how the feathers of the Base Shape are larger than the feathers that embellish it. The embellishing feathers are longer and slimmer, distinguishing them from the Base Shape.

You can see in Turquoise Sampler below that there's very little contrast between the Triple Paisley Base

Shape and the feathers in the two examples (left and center below). The final example (below right) illustrates how the Triple Paisley Base Shape is enhanced by the ample contrast between the Base Shape and the feather embellishment. All three are lovely, but I find the one on the right most pleasing.

Question Mark Base Shapes

In these two examples both Standard Feathers and Dream Feathers are used to embellish the Question Mark Base Shape (page 74).

Dream Feathers

Standard Feathers

When sketching and doodling, there may be times when you like one side of the design better than the other. Such is the case with the Dream Feathers example shown above. I like both sides individually, but not

together; the horizontal midline is not consistent on both sides. This is partly because the Question Mark Base Shape is not a mirror image; one side is concave, and the other is convex.

However, if I were to use this design in a quilt, I would still like both sides to more closely resemble one another. To accomplish this I would do the following:

1. Draw the Base Shape either using a template or freehand.

2. Draw the upper, lower, and middle horizontal guidelines. Note that I did not place the middle horizontal line directly in the middle of the Base Shape. This was purely arbitrary. If necessary, chalk in vertical guidelines to delineate the outer limits of the design.

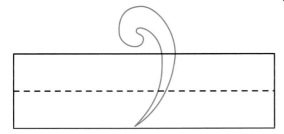

3. Proceed to create Dream Feathers. Now the design is more balanced and more pleasing because both sides have five feathers in the first shell set and there is a consistent horizontal midpoint. Each side is different, but the eye is not aware of the differences.

Here are three more adaptations of the original design. You can quickly see the versatility of the Dream Feather technique.

These first two motifs would fit nicely in a border. On the first one, I raised the upper horizontal guideline.

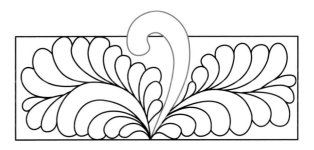

For the second one I added a second plume of Dream Feathers to help balance the design.

Both of these designs would lend themselves to a mirrored image, creating a stylized butterfly that would be beautiful on a wide border. See the Butterflies and Hearts chapter (pages 48–53) for more information on this adaptation.

For the third adaptation of the original motif, I slanted the bottom right guideline as shown by the line on the right, forcing the feathers in another direction. You can easily see how this could be designed to fit into a triangular space.

In every instance, you can choose to begin with a pattern or you can simply chalk in the Base Shape and stitch the feathers freehand.

The Curled Paisley Base Shape

The Curled Paisley Base Shape (page 71) has an unexpected starting point. Here is how it is drawn.

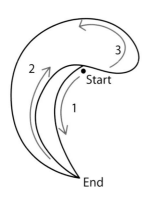

Both of these designs start with a Curled Paisley Base Shape with Dream Feathers on the right side and Standard Feathers on the left that developed into Dream Feathers. Simply by manipulating the perimeters, the shape changes and adapts to the space available.

This ornate design starts with the Curled Paisley and combines both Standard and Dream Feathers. This design lends itself to unusual or oddly shaped spaces.

S-Curve Base Shape Variations

The S-Curve Base Shape (page 72) is extremely versatile and undoubtedly the shape I use more often than any other.

The motif below is shown with Standard Feathers on both sides.

This design starts with Dream Feathers on the right and Standard Feathers on the left. However on the left side, the Standard Feathers have eventually become the base for branching into the Dream Feather.

This next variation combines Standard Feathers on the left and elegant flowing Dream Feathers on the right.

Remember: The Standard Feather uses the Base Shape as a spine; Dream Feathers branch away from the Base Shape and build on previous feathers.

Cornucopia Base Shape Variations

Here we have three treatments of the Cornucopia Base Shape (page 73).

This preliminary sketch using Standard Feathers is somewhat uninteresting.

Combining Standard and Dream Feathers adds interest.

Dream Feathers on both sides of the Base Shape create a beautiful motif.

Below is the mirror image of the same design, creating a Butterfly motif.

Single Line Designs

So far we have dealt with shapes, but these line designs are so lovely and versatile that I wanted to share them as well.

The S-Shaped Base Line

Exercise

1. Draw a simple S-Shaped Base Line. Curl in the ends. Chalk in a center line.

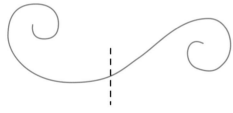

2. Beginning at the center marking, stitch Standard Feathers on the outside edge of the line. Repeat for the other side. The feathers go in opposite directions, emanating from the center.

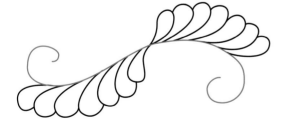

Look at this same concept with the feathers on the inside of the curve. Isn't it amazing how even the slightest change can create such a dramatic difference? A Pumpkin Seed Base Shape was used in the center instead of a chalked line. Even changing the curled end to a paisley shape affects the final outcome.

You can also vary the sizes of the feathers as shown here. Notice how the Standard Feathers develop into Dream Feathers as they float off the original Base Line.

Consider other embellishments. Look at the lovely result when adding Wrought Iron (page 22) in conjunction with feathers.

The S-Line is embellished with Dream Feathers in a completely different orientation. Dream Feathers flow away from the line rather than use it as a base.

Try the Dream Feather at each end of the design. The original S-Shaped Base Line was drawn first. Standard Feathers were placed along the line. Upon reaching the end of the line, I simply kept going with the Dream Feathering. How ornate will you get?

S-Lines can be placed end-to-end to create a beautiful swag.

Here I continued to draw Dream Feathers.

These motifs are also lovely when stood on end. Turn any of these S-Shaped Base Line designs to a vertical orientation to see how they could be used in a row on a border.

Question Mark Base Line

This is such a pretty design. It reminds me of an old fashioned quill. These three designs are variations of the Question Mark Base Line.

Simple Question Mark Base Line with Standard Feathers.

Paisley shape on the end with Dream Feathers

This design starts with a curl on the end with Dream Feathers oriented in a different direction.

Wrought Iron

This simple line is a great embellishment on feathered motifs. It also fills narrow borders nicely. It is a Question Mark Base Line with multiple curves.

Exercise

1. Begin with a Question Mark.

2. Backtrack as indicated by the arrows.

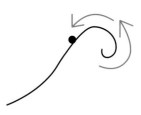

3. Curl in the opposite direction.

4. Continue in this manner to create a vine.

This is a versatile design that works well in a variety of sizes of borders as well as a background fill, as shown in TURQUOISE SAMPLER.

Feathered Wrought Iron

Feathered Wrought Iron is another Single Line design. It combines the Wrought Iron Curls with Standard Feathers. It would make a great background fill as is or with added flowers and tendrils for a more folk-art effect. It is a great design for a narrow band.

Exercise

1. Start with a Question Mark Base Line and backtrack to the origination point.

2. Feather the outside curve.

3. Proceed forward with another curl in the opposite direction.

4. Backtrack and once again feather the outside edge.

5. Add more Wrought Iron curls to make the design even more interesting.

Try this same concept but use a combination of Standard and Dream Feathers. Add more curls or even some leaves. The BORDER SAMPLER quilt (page 32) has several smaller borders that use the Wrought Iron embellishment. I also think that this could have some freehand allover possibilities as well. What will you try first?

Furls & Flourishes

In case you need more stimulation, let's look at some variations. Remember, you can use any of the following designs in whatever sizes fit your needs.

Embellishing the Base Shapes

We can create even more designs by altering the Base Shape, changing the feathers to other embellishments, or by using a combination of these techniques.

Here is the Paisley Base Shape, but this time the tip has been altered.

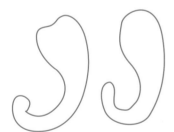

See how the design is changed simply by curving the tail?

Making the shape longer and skinnier or shorter and fatter also creates an entirely new design.

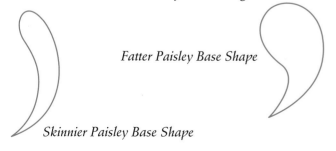

Fatter Paisley Base Shape

Skinnier Paisley Base Shape

Look what happens to the simple S-Base Shape if we make it fatter.

When the S-Base Shape is enlarged, a second element can be added to the interior, here with a String of Pearls fill.

Add the feathers and you have created pure elegance like this design. Doesn't it remind you of an elegant bird? Can't you just see it as a medallion center of a whole cloth? (See Medallions, pages 46–47.)

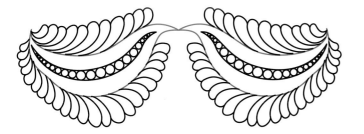

When you draw the shapes freehand, you will automatically create variations in the structure.

When you create a shape variation that you want to save, you might consider making a template for future use.

SHADOW TRAPUNTO (page 56), detail, showing a fatter S-Curve Base Shape with String of Pearls in the center

Here are two variations of the Chubby S-Curve Base Shape.

The first is enhanced by a mirror-image orientation.

The second is a different rendition of the Elegant Bird.

Here is a nice Chubby Cornucopia Base Shape with the addition of String of Pearls and Dream Feathers. It reminds me of the Cheshire Cat's grin and I smile every time I see it!

The Cornucopia Base Shape does some amazing things when its top is manipulated, as shown in this example.

Imagine all of the possibilities once you start altering the Base Shapes. Each of these variations will produce a new look and endless possibilities for embellishing. In addition, many designs will change appearance just by rotating them to a different viewing perspective.

Embellishment Options

While this book is about feathers in general and specifically my Dream Feathers, the Base Shapes also lend themselves to other applications and embellishments such as Curls, Tendrils, Wrought Iron, and String of Pearls.

Curls are fun, especially if you are uncomfortable about backtracking.

Exercise

1. Begin with a Base Shape as usual. (A modified Question Mark Base Shape was used here.) Curl away from the shape.

Step 1

2. Return to the Base Shape echoing the first curl.

Step 2

3. Curl back out, ending on the last stitched line.

Step 3

4. Again echo back to the Base Shape.

Step 4

5. Continue along the Base Shape with Standard, or, as in this example, Dream Feathers.

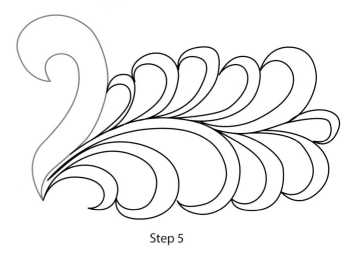

Step 5

Curls would be quite interesting if you made the echoed lines large enough to fill with a String of Pearls as in this example.

Tendrils allow you to reach into small spaces for balance. They are particularly effective if you are using a leaf as the Base Shape but also add nice accents to feathers.

Tendrils

Wrought Iron embellishment adds a whole new dimension.

Wrought Iron

Tendrils and Wrought Iron embellishments are particularly helpful in reaching into odd areas where other motifs won't work.

String of Pearls can embellish either the feathers or interiors of the Base Shapes. This design uses pearls in the interior as well as an embellishment on the feathers.

Not all designs that you sketch will be useable.

The one above really has too many things happening on it to be considered as a viable design. However, it

does illustrate just how many different applications could be considered as embellishment on a single Base Shape—a Chubby Paisley, in this case.

If I were to use this design, I would choose one element and carry it through. Since I like the String of Pearls, I might end up with a design that looks something like this.

This is significantly better than the original doodling, showing why I continue to encourage you to doodle. The original was not pretty at all, but this final design is worthy of consideration in a quilt.

Here are two more embellished designs. These would both be options if you were using an organic theme in the quilt.

Tendril and Wrought Iron embellishments

Tendril, Wrought Iron, and Leaf embellishments

Pomegranate

Two Crescent Base Shapes (page 75) facing one another are the basis for this design decorated with Standard Feathers, Pearls, and Wrought Iron.

Don't dismiss the possibility that hearts, flowers, or even stars might be just what are needed. I am sure you will come up with even more ideas to be used as fillers and embellishments.

As you play with Base Shapes, manipulating and adding your own signature, be sure to make a template. Again, I encourage you to maintain a journal. You are going to love some of your new designs. You'll be amazed at the multitude of possible variations and manipulations as you keep track of your doodling.

Leaf Base

In this design, a leaf shape is used as the base. It creates a unique mood that may be just what a quilt needs.

Additional Design Ideas

Some of the following designs are quite involved. However, armed with the information presented thus far and with careful study, you will be able to discern how the design was created. Remember, they all begin with a Base Shape and have been manipulated or embellished, or both.

Crescent

The top of the Cornucopia Base Shape was the inspiration for this lovely motif that lends itself to manipulation and ornamentation. Two Crescent Base Shapes slightly overlapped to create this new Base Shape.

a.

These three samples show progressively more detailed embellishments of the Question Mark Base Shape—starting with a simple vertical orientation (a), then a more horizontal orientation (b), and finally a more embellished and boxy version (c) with the Dream Feather embellishing playing a more important role in the overall design.

c.

b.

Photos are details from
TURQUOISE SAMPLER
(full quilt not shown).

Borders & Swags

Now that you have created all of these lovely motifs, it is time to actually use them. This is where the real magic occurs.

Of course, any of the designs in this book or that you have created will stand alone. For instance, they would be beautiful in the spacer blocks of an Irish Chain or the centers of Double Wedding Ring blocks. But these beauties will do more than that. Let's explore some possibilities.

Spacing Motifs on Borders

How many times have you purchased a stencil or quilting pattern only to discover that it doesn't quite fit the dimensions of your quilt? You stand with stencil in hand knowing that it would be lovely on the quilt, but the quilt's dimensions are divisible by 5 and the stencil is a multiple of 3". With some simple paper folding techniques you can determine just exactly what size to make your own personal designs.

Placing individual motifs on borders can be problematic, so we will start there. The spacing is usually the stumbling block. Often, finding a design that fits the dimensions of the quilt poses a problem. By designing your own patterns you will always have a perfect fit.

There are many ways to solve this dilemma. One I like to use is a simple folded paper technique. Once again that roll of newsprint comes to the rescue.

Cut a piece of newsprint the length of your border. (I sometimes exclude the corners and put a related motif in each corner instead.) Fold the paper in half and in half again. Continue folding until you have a section that will accommodate your selected design. Eight sections are usually ample for divisions. Sometimes I stop at four.

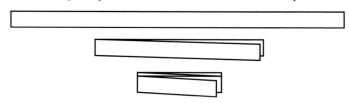

Open the paper and place it on the quilt border. Using the fold lines for reference, chalk in the divisions. You now have guidelines for each motif in your border and no math was harmed in the process.

For other divisions, begin by folding the paper in thirds first. If you fold in half again, you will get six divisions. Or if you fold in thirds a second time, you will get nine.

For five divisions, place the first motif in the center of the border. Place the second and third motifs at each end, and center the fourth and fifth motifs between. In this instance, you would not need the folded paper guide.

The folded paper can be used as a guide for placement of individual designs, but it can also be used to create continuous designs. Base Shapes and Folded Paper Applications (pages 36–45) provides directions for creating designs using various folded-paper techniques.

Swags

When placed end-to-end, the S-Curve Base Shape makes beautiful swags. Experiment with mirror images or try flipping the shape. Each manipulation will create a unique design because the S-Curve is not necessarily symmetrical; both halves are different.

These two examples illustrate creating a ribbon design with the S-Curve Base Shape.

*The Base Shape is oriented in a mirror image;
a String of Pearls enhances the center.*

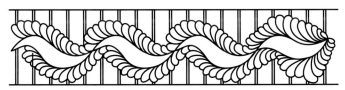

*A ribbon effect develops when the shape is placed end-to-end.
The addition of Double Piano Keys sets off the design perfectly.*

These two designs and others are stitched out on the BORDER SAMPLER (page 32).

Here, the Crescent Base Shape is manipulated. Several of these could create lovely swags.

With simple manipulations, each of these designs will produce a variety of similar motifs. A mirror image of a single unit creates the basis for swags in a border. If the angle of the mirrored image is decreased, you can create a design that would fit in blocks in the body of a quilt or in cornerstones.

Exercise

Trace any of the single designs shown here and see just how many variations you can create. Align them end-to-end; place them back-to-back; add tendrils; use curls instead of feathers; see if you can create a design that would fit into a setting triangle. Try starting with a fatter Crescent Base Shape, allowing you to embellish within the shape. There are so many possibilities, it's impossible to even begin to list them all here.

This set of designs (page 31), which uses the Crescent Base Shape, clearly illustrates how using my Base Shape method unifies a quilting plan. Any one of these designs could be placed side-by-side for a border. Single designs could be used in individual blocks in the same quilt. By changing the angle of the Base Shape, the designs can accommodate the space of a setting triangle. The Base Shape provides a clear starting point for the quilting throughout the quilt creating cohesive harmony.

The BORDER SAMPLER shows a variety of applications. From top to bottom:
Row 1: Dream Feathers with Pumpkin Seed start
Row 2: Single Shell Sets
Rows 3, 4, 5 & 6: Variations of Wrought Iron
Row 7: S-Curve Base Shape mirrored and repeated
Row 8: S-Curve Base Shape set end-to-end
Row 9: Crescent Base Shape mirrored and repeated with Double Piano Keys backfill

BORDER SAMPLER, 33" x 38½", made by the author

Going in Circles

Seeing a border of feathers flowing completely around a quilt is beautiful, but nestling the final feather into the beginning feathers can be a bit tricky.

One way I have accomplished this is to chalk in the first few feathers. I then start stitching on the final feather in the first shell set. I stitch around the border, and pay close attention to the spacing as I approach that beginning space. I use the original markings as guides to nestle the feathers.

1. Chalk in a series of beginning feathers. This should consist of two shell sets of feathers.

2. Begin stitching on the final feather of the first shell set of chalked-in feathers. Begin the second set of feathers on the second feather as shown in the example above right. The red lines indicate the chalked-in guides, and the black lines indicate the actual stitching. For clarity, the lines are not on top of each other, but you would stitch on the chalked lines. Once you have used the chalked lines for guidance, erase them.

Note carefully the points where the stitching begins on both the right and left sides. They are not where you might expect them to be!

3. Continue stitching around the entire border free hand. (We will discuss how to go around corners shortly.) The dotted red lines indicate the chalked lines that have been erased.

4. Adjust the spacing of the feathers as you approach the beginning stitching. If you are uncomfortable just eyeing the spacing, you can also chalk in the last few feathers, but it won't take you long to learn that you can simply eyeball this. The red lines indicate the final stitches as they are adjusted to nestle into the beginning stitching.

Another way to handle feathered borders is to start with a Base Shape at the center of each border. The feathering flows out from the center to the end of each border. At the corners, chalk in a diagonal guideline for ending the feathers as shown here in red.

Diagonal corner reconciliation

Another option is to extend the borders to the outer edges of the quilt in the classic butted border style, often seen in vintage Amish and Welsh quilts.

Butted corner reconciliation

I have also made Base Shapes at the center of the top and bottom borders, and reconciled the garlands at the centers of the side borders.

Side border center reconciliation

There are as many solutions are there are quilters! I am sure you can come up with many more. For instance, try Base Shapes in each corner with the garlands meeting at the center of each border.

Turning Corners

Now let's talk a bit more about going around corners. It looks rather mysterious, but when broken down into individual steps it's really quite easy.

As you approach a corner, remember that we still have to maintain the deep curves found in Dream Feathers. This is accomplished by positioning every shell set beyond the middle horizontal plane of the border. If you are comfortable doing so, you can just eyeball this, but you can also chalk in a guideline as shown in red.

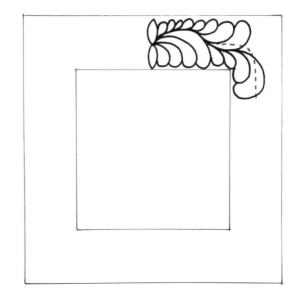

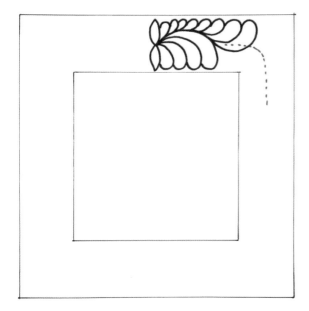

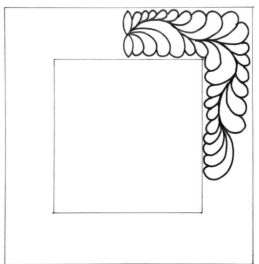

The next step is to stitch around the inside of the corner adding feathers until one crosses over the horizontal plane, as shown in the first figure to the right.

Proceed with feathers on the outside edge to complete the turn, as shown in the second figure to the right.

This process works equally well if you need to stitch on the outside of the border first. Here, I made the outer shell set first and then stitched the smaller, inner feathers, as shown in the third figure to the right.

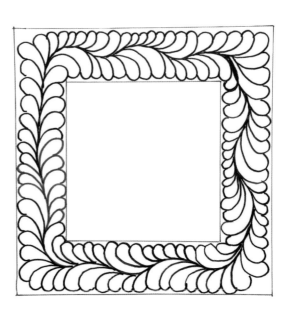

Base Shapes & Folded Paper Applications

I wondered what would happen if I drew Base Shapes onto folded paper. I began playing with this concept and a whole new dimension was revealed. I started with simply folding paper into quarters and went on from there with a myriad of variations. The more I folded, the more intricate the designs became.

I was transported to my childhood fascination with kaleidoscopes and cutting out snowflakes in elementary school. Oh, how I loved seeing beautiful designs emerge as I twirled that tube of colored glass shards or unfolded the cut paper.

I confess, I am just as thrilled with that magical moment now as I was when I was ten. This process is very addicting and never-ending. So, are you ready for a new adventure?

These paper-folding exercises may just be my all-time favorite thing to do. So many designs and so little time to execute them! Creating folded paper designs is much like adding to your fabric stash—you will create more designs than you can possibly use.

Do not obsess about the beauty or perfection of your designs when you are doing these exercises. Consider them playtime.

Once you have designs that you want to pursue, there are several ways to get them from paper to quilt. Sometimes I will just create a template of the Base Shape. Using my drawing as a placement reference, I simply chalk in the Base Shape and fill in the feathers freehand.

Other times I will make a template of just one repeat and then lay out the entire design, again using the original drawing for reference. Still other times, I have found that it is best to make a complete template and mark the quilt entirely before quilting.

When I begin quilting, I get into the rhythm of the design and automatically make adjustments, smoothing out little wobbles and other imperfections that occured during the design process.

Paper Folding Methods

We are going to make designs by folding paper. Using your handy-dandy supply of newsprint, begin by cutting a square of paper. For this set of exercises try a 10"–12" square. When actually creating designs for a specific quilt, the paper should be the same size as the block or space for which you are creating the design.

Method One

We will begin with the simplest paper folding technique.

1. Fold the paper in half and then into quarters.

2. Select a Base Shape.

3. Position the Base Shape so that portions of it fall on the folds. If you do not have the design touching folds, you will end up with four separate pieces of paper!

4. Cut out the shape to produce a template for your design.

Here is a Cornucopia Base Shape placed on a quartered square.

And this is the paper cut out as well as the template made from the paper pattern.

The Method One stitched version is shown below.

Even the simplest of variations produces more designs. Still using Method One, I oriented the Cornucopia Base Shape in two different positions to produce similar designs. Each is interesting in its own right.

A second way to use this method is to fold on the diagonals rather than the horizontal and vertical planes. That is what I did to create this next design. One quarter of this design would perfectly fit into a setting tri-

angle and half of the design could be positioned end-to-end to create a swag for a border. Notice how a single Wrought Iron motif reaches into the empty space.

Method Two

1. Start with the square and again fold into quarters.

2. Fold on the diagonal, aligning the folds.

3. Draw a Base Shape, making sure that portions of the design fall on the folds of the paper.

This is the paper and the final template.

The Method Two stitched version is shown below.

And here is the Method Three block stitched.

Method Three

1. Once again start with a square.

2. Fold in half diagonally.

3. Fold into thirds. Your paper should look like this.

4. Select a Base shape and proceed as before.

This method produces an even more intricate design. The paper pattern is on the left and the plastic template is on the right.

And finally…

Method Four

Fold the square of paper on both diagonals, and then into thirds for an intricate, lacy pattern as shown below. I just eyeball folding into thirds, but if you want absolute precision, this is a 60-degree angle.

Here are the cut out and the template.

And finally, the stitched Method Four version.

To finish this CORNUCOPIA SAMPLER, individual Cornucopia Base Shapes were used in the corner-stones.

The interior feathered borders began with a single Cornucopia Base Shape in the center of the borders.

Here is the full CORNUCOPIA SAMPLER. A balanced design is achieved by using the same Base Shape throughout the entire quilt.

CORNUCOPIA SAMPLER,
38" x 38",
made by the author

Paper Folding with Feathers

The previous methods produce what I call Line Designs. They stand on their own without further embellishment. However, this is only the beginning. Perhaps you want to have feathers around the motif. If so, you will need to include the feathers in the original folded-paper process.

Exercise

Begin by choosing one of the methods described above. Make a smaller Base Shape to allow room for the feathers. Add feathers to the Base Shape. Remember: At least part of the design must touch folded edges.

This photo shows a very skinny S-Curve Base Shape used as a foundation using Method One for a fully-feathered design.

For Marguerite's quilt, PRETTY IN PINK (page 64), I began with 12" squares of paper, since that is the size of the blocks in the quilt. I used Method One to create the stylized Butterfly designs on the right (shown stitched on page 52).

It's fun to see how simply placing the Base Shape differently creates a whole new design. The next two designs (page 42) use the S-Curve Base Shape and Method One, and yet they create totally different designs, each one unique and beautiful. The folds are oriented

the same in these two samples, but you can see the different orientation of the Base Shape.

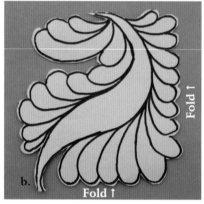

When opened we have two very distinct designs.

A word of caution: Playing with the folded paper technique is very addictive. Once you start adding various embellishments, it is truly mind-boggling, and you will be going through rolls of newsprint very quickly.

I suggest that you make a notation on each design regarding which paper folding method you used for future reference. You may want to revisit a design and will be glad that you have that information.

I have found that when using smaller squares of paper, Method Four does not lend itself well to adding feathers. If you want to use this method for a feathered design, start with a larger square of paper. I started with a 24" square for this design.

This is a spectacular design stitched out as shown on DREAM FEATHER EXPLOSION (page 43). This quilt was completely marked before I loaded it onto the machine. Yes, including a ¾" crosshatch for the background!

DREAM FEATHER EXPLOSION,
35½" x 38", made by the author

Things to Remember about Paper Folding

At least part of the design must touch the folds of the paper or your design will fall apart.

Use paper folding to make Line Designs or to add feathers or other embellishments.

I used several of the paper folding methods to create the designs for Chris Milodragovich's quilt, FOR THE QUILTER (pages 62–63). Here is the template I used to create the motif for the spacer blocks. I used the same template for the setting triangles.

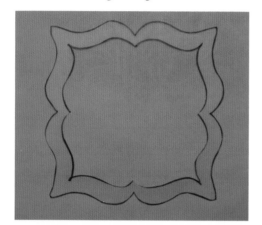

The framework was chalked in and the feathering was done freehand.

All of the designs were based on a modified S-Curve Base Shape. Here is how that translated into a swag for the deep 13" borders.

The template

The pattern

FOR THE QUILTER, *border detail (above) and spacer blocks detail (left)*

The same Base Shape was slightly modified to create the corner connections.

FOR THE QUILTER, detail

The Results

Here are some patterns all created using a variety of paper folding methods. These all began with the versatile S-Curve Base Shape.

Medallions

There is just something about wholecloth quilts that thrills our souls. Their elegant simplicity draws us in for a closer look. It is then that we discover the beautiful center medallion and the ancillary designs that pull everything together.

You can use any of the designs in the book or that you have created as stand-alone center medallions. Both Line Designs and fully feathered designs work well as a center medallion. They just have to be sized to fit the quilt. Here is how I do that.

Sizing Center Medallion Designs

Determine the size and shape of your medallion. I have found that 24" or larger works quite well.

Cut a square of paper to the desired size.

Choose a paper folding method. The more divisions you have, the more intricate your designs will be.

Choose a Base Shape either from the Glossary of Shapes or one that you have created.

Draw the shape onto the folded paper. Make a template of just the Base Shape for use throughout the quilt. Remember: Your design must touch the folded sides of the paper or it will fall apart!

Create a design with only the Base Shape, or add the feathers. Keep the Base Shape small enough to allow for the feathering to be done within your desired medallion space.

Using your method of preference, transfer the design to the fabric.

Your medallion design is now ready to stitch and embellish.

Many of the designs and Base Shapes found in this book could be used as a jumping off point for center medallions. And you will most certainly develop more of your own.

Unifying Quilting Designs

Look again at the Elegant Bird designs (pages 24–25). This is one of my favorite designs, so I used it for reference to draw this medallion.

Since the S-Curve Base Shape was used as the starting point, using that same shape throughout the quilt provides harmony and lyricism overall.

The Elegant Bird as a repeated stand-alone motif would be a lovely border to accompany this medallion. Back them with Double Piano Keys, curved or straight-line cross-hatching, or simply let them speak for themselves.

Another border possibility would be to use alternating repeats of one section of the center medallion.

Notice how a portion of the design is ready for a triangular application.

Breaking out the original Base Shape, or perhaps just a portion of it, gives you the basis for borders and corners. These designs would also complement a medallion featuring the Elegant Bird.

By now you should be able to see how these Base Shapes become the basis for your quilting designs. Choose any Base Shape as the starting point. By manipulation, it can be used in blocks, as a medallion, in setting triangles, and in borders. The use of a single Base Shape embellished with feathering or other embellishments of your choice unifies the entire quilt.

No more wondering, "How do I quilt this?" No more disparate, unrelated motifs in your quilts. Simply choose a Base Shape and let it work its magic.

Butterflies & Hearts

Butterflies

This design began as an experiment. I wanted to vary the length of the feather within a confined area such as a border.

I began with the drawing on the left. I liked how the feathers seemed to emanate from a seam line and created a shell. The idea developed further with embellishments. I liked what was happening here.

But wait. What if I mirrored these? Of course, I then had to repeat the design to see how it looked. This is the result. These are still using a straight line as a guide.

Then I drew them without a guideline, creating a more flowing design. All of these are spineless and continuous. Remember, we are creating feathers without first marking or stitching a spine. These feathers build on one another.

This was when I realized that I was creating stylized Butterflies, and not only do they look great connected, they also are beautiful as stand-alone motifs. Here is a Butterfly using a reshaped Question Mark Base Shape.

These designs began with the Question Mark Base Line. Notice that for this variation, the Base Line is turned upside down from the way we originally drew it in the chapter on Single Line Designs (pages 20–23).

Exercise

1. Start with two Crescent Base Shapes to form the flower-like embellishments, then continue with a Question Mark Base Line.

2. Draw a second line, overlapping the first and add a second flower embellishment.

3. Add feathers. With a little planning and careful back-tracking, this can be done continuously.

Here the same design has been treated with Dream Feathers at the top.

As you can see, these motifs can also be stand-alone designs, and they fit anywhere because they are free-hand. You can adapt them to your space simply by extending the feathers into hard-to-reach areas, or by adding Tendril or Wrought Iron embellishments.

Exercise

To draw the basic Butterfly:

1. Draw a line to represent a seam line or the center of the Butterfly. Draw a second line as a guide for the side of the motif (the dashed red line).

2. Draw a five-unit Dream Feather, or use any number that fits your space. Start with a small feather. Continue until the final feather touches the outer red line.

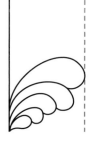

3. Feather the final feather with smaller feathers.

4. Echo back to the center line.

5. Continue along the center line and you will have a beautiful border.

6. Repeat on the other side to create Butterflies. A seam line works nicely as the center. Simply stitch on either side of the seam.

Hearts

Generally, any shape that is curved more or less like a "C" will produce a Butterfly when placed back-to-back, but if you place them facing one another, they will produce a Heart.

These two illustrations start out the same with Question Mark Base Lines and Wrought Iron, but the upper illustration uses Standard Feathers and the lower image illustrates it with Dream Feathers. Isn't it amazing how such a simple thing as changing from Standard Feathers to Dream Feathers creates a different image?

Now is the time to look back at preceding chapters to discover other designs that might lend themselves to creating Butterflies and Hearts. Here are some to get you started.

A modified Paisley Base Shape is the basis for these two designs oriented to create Hearts. One design sports flowing Standard Feathers, while the other features Dream Feathers. Is it getting easier to tell the difference between the two types of feathers?

Standard Feathers

Dream Feathers

A very simple Paisley Base Shape provides the foundation for this design, elegant in its simplicity.

The Curled Paisley Base Shape combined with feathers and a String of Pearls spreads its wings in the beauty shown above right. Strings of Pearls are used to emphasize the Base Shape creating this Butterfly design.

I had the honor of quilting Marguerite Shattuck's hand-pieced quilt, PRETTY IN PINK (page 64). Since the quilt is a sampler, I chose to create a sampling of Butterflies and Hearts. Following is a Heart design and a detail of the quilt showing the design stitched out.

Repeating half of these motifs
end-to-end creates an effective
border pattern.

PRETTY IN PINK, detail.
Full quilt on page 64.
Design patterns shown on page 41.

Let's round out this chapter with one more Butterfly idea. A mirror image of this design is shown as a single unit on page 17. I'm not sure which way I like it best.

Oriented like this, it reminds me of an iris. When mirrored, it turns into a Butterfly.

No matter how it is positioned, it is an effective design.

Hearts and Butterflies are so much fun to design. I could make dozens of them. But I don't want to deprive you of the fun of making them for yourself! Just choose a Base Shape and start doodling. Soon you will have more designs than you have quilts to be quilted!

Wouldn't this reflection be lovely in a border?

Other Uses for the Designs

As I created these designs, it occurred to me that many of them could be used for techniques other than basic quilting. I just couldn't resist playing with them. The examples here all began with this same template, using the S-Curve Base Shape, but oh my, what different results.

For years I have wanted to add color to quilted pieces. I did some initial experimentation with less than happy results. However, after having read Irena Blum's book, *Quilts of a Different Color* (AQS, 2008), I had to try it again. I was lucky to see Irena's initial foray into this technique and am thrilled at how much fun it is.

This piece is my first attempt at the technique, but it won't be my last.

PAINTED LADY, 31" x 21", made by the author

This quilt started out as a solid color in the middle that I first quilted. I then painted it using a variety of media including watercolor pencils and crayons, water-soluble oil pastels, and colored pencils. The background fill consists of a combination of Dream Feathers, Wrought Iron, and Tendrils.

Painted Lady, detail

As I played with these designs, I could see that many of them would lend themselves to appliqué. I asked my friend, Myrna Nyberg, to try her hand at this design. I added the quilting and other finishing touches. As you can see, this opens up a whole new realm of possibilities. An appliqué for the center of a medallion quilt would be beautiful. All of the quilting would incorporate the Base Shape used in designing the appliqué.

Appliqué Sampler,
24" x 24",
appliquéd by Myrna Nyberg,
Missoula, Montana,
constructed and quilted by the author

Finally, I used the very same template to produce the center medallion of this SHADOW TRAPUNTO whole-cloth quilt. I oriented the template in the same direction around a center axis, producing a subtle feeling of motion. The S-Curve Base Shape was used for the border applications and a commercial template was used for the background fill.

SHADOW TRAPUNTO,
32½" x 36",
made by the author

Finis

But not the end!

And so on it goes. With just a few basic shapes in hand there are endless possibilities for bringing life and beauty to your quilting. From the most basic to the ornately elegant, each design will be fresh and exciting. It is my hope that you have found new inspiration among these pages.

At some point, a book has to end, and I haven't shared anywhere near all the designs that are in my sketch books, nor all the ideas that are in my head. But your fun has just begun. Your imagination will take you far beyond what is here. This is by no means an exhaustive resource for the possibilities, although discovering all your new designs may be exhausting!

Don't forget your sketch pad or journal every time you sit down or leave the house. You may not always use it, but I promise you if you don't have it, that will be the time you want it the most.

Now it is time for you to create your own unique Dream Feathers.

Gallery

BOSTON COMMON, 82" x 88", made by the author

Cornucopia Sampler, 38¼" x 38¼", made by the author

*POINTS AND DOTS, 72" x 92",
made by Patricia J. Cross, Missoula, Montana.
First-time feathers done on her home machine!*

FOR THE QUILTER, 84" x 84", made by Christine Milodragovich, Missoula, Montana, quilted by the author

*PRETTY IN PINK, 77" x 77", made by Marguerite Shattuck,
Missoula, Montana, quilted by the author*

*REMEMBERING: BELLE'S STAR, 59" x 67", made by the author
in honor of her mother-in-law, Belle Kalberg*

SPRING DREAMS, 49" x 49", made and quilted by Robin Hall, Missoula, Montana. Adapted from GARDEN COMFORT by Mimi Dietrich. First-time feathers done on her home machine!

Glossary of Shapes

The Base Shapes included here are commonly used shapes. They are found in contemporary quilting as well as in ancient architectural and textile applications.

When I want a new motif or just need an infusion of fresh ideas, I often turn to my camera. You may be surprised where you can find inspiration. Consider a stroll through the oldest sections of your local cemetery, where you will find classical motifs of all kinds. One may be just the inspiration for a bold new design.

Take pictures of ornamentation on historic buildings. Oftentimes you will see beautiful scroll work or wrought iron gates that trigger a design concept.

I also avail myself of publications on architecture and textiles. One of my favorites is *The Grammar of Ornament* by Owen Jones (The Ivy Press, 2001). This publication is overflowing with a comprehensive discussion of ornamentation throughout history. In fact its cover has a design on it that prompted my exploration culminating in the creation of the Dream Feather.

Another resource that I often turn to is *Pattern Motifs, A Sourcebook* by Graham Leslie McCallum (Batsford, 2006). I have spent many pleasant hours poring over the hundreds, perhaps thousands, of illustrations in this book.

The vast majority of my design books come from Dover publications. Among many titles I have is *The Enschede Catalog of Typographic Borders and Ornaments*. This book is simply beautiful to peruse and full of inspiration.

Look for books on Baroque designs. Islamic designs also provide inspiration as do calligraphic and tile designs. I have used Dover's *Traditional Floral Designs and Motifs for Artists and Craftspeople* frequently, and the leaf designs were the inspiration for my experimentation using leaves as Base Shapes. Another inspirational resource for me is Anita Shackleford's *Infinite Feathers Quilting Designs* (AQS, 2002) and template (www.anitashackleford.com).

No matter the source, doodle and sketch. Experiment. When I find shapes I want to explore, I will do a quick sketch in my journal and note the source. That way I can quickly find the original reference.

The following pages contain Base Shapes for your use. They are arbitrary in nature. Simply put, any shape that even vaguely resembles these Base Shapes will be fantastic; consider them as guides rather than concrete patterns. However, if you are feeling the need to have shapes that you can use just as is, these will get you started.

Paisley Base Shape

The Paisley Base Shape started it all.

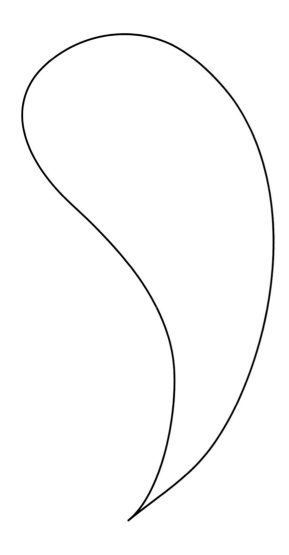

You may discover that you need other Paisley Base Shapes—maybe a fatter, squattier Paisley. You might want to start here.

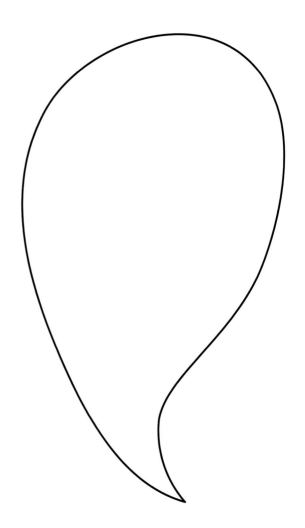

Triple Paisley Base Shape

The elegant Triple Paisley provides the basis for a multitude of embellishing opportunities with Standard or Dream Feathers or a combination of both. It is also a beautiful stand-alone motif. Perhaps you have an area that isn't large enough for a full-blown design. Choose the Triple Paisley as your main shape.

Using the Base Shape alone, combined with the more decorated version in larger areas, will provide the desired continuity on the quilt. This design works best if you change the scale of the embellishments. Keep the Triple Paisley larger than the added feathering.

Pumpkin Seed &
Teardrop Base Shapes

The Pumpkin Seed is just two arcs, joined. Technically, it is the result of two overlapping circles. Two Pumpkin Seeds stacked one above the other provide the perfect base for establishing Dream Feathers on a border. The Pumpkin Seed Base Shape can be modified to become a Teardrop, another versatile shape to work with.

Curled Paisley Base Shape

I love the Curled Paisley. It is unusual and calls attention to itself. The larger shape invites some wonderful interior embellishing such as a String of Pearls. Experiment with variations, perhaps curling the top more deeply or making the original crescent fatter.

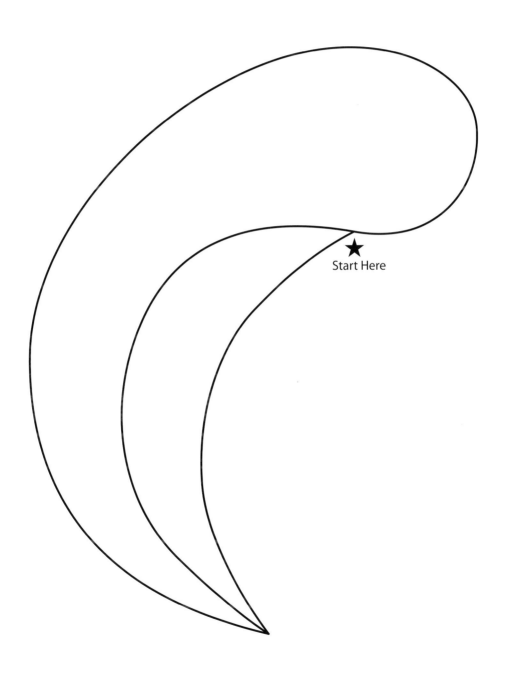

★
Start Here

S-Curve Base Shape

The S-Curve may be the most versatile of all the Base Shapes. It forms the basis for Hearts and Butterflies. Its fluidity adds elegance and grace to any quilt. It is not a mirror image of itself so it creates some interesting possibilities. However, you could make it a mirror image by tracing it halfway, flipping and tracing that same end again. This produces a totally different design and may just be the basis for some gorgeous patterns.

Placed end-to-end, the S-Curve Base Shape will create a beautiful ribbon that can be embellished with feathers. Two skinny shapes placed vertically with just their bases touching create a beautiful vase. How will you fill it? Feathers? Ferns? Flowers? A single teardrop?

Cornucopia Base Shape

Fill the Cornucopia with feathers. Lay it on its side. Orient it vertically. It lends itself to a variety of treatments.

Chubby Cornucopia Base Shape

The Chubby Cornucopia is so much fun to work with. You can add lots of different embellishments—String of Pearls, for instance. Experiment with placing a small motif of Dream Feathers inside the shape.

Question Mark Base Shape

The Question Mark is basically a variation of the Paisley Base Shape. (Or perhaps it's a variation of the S-Curve Base Shape as demonstrated by the figure at the bottom of the page. You decide.) Either way it is a wonderful shape. It can be used singly but don't forget the design possibilities when placing two shapes back-to-back or facing one another.

Crescent Base Shape

The Crescent Base Shape can be used in a variety of ways. The top of the Cornucopia Base Shape is two Crescent Base Shapes. One of my favorite designs using this shape is the Pomegranate shown on page 28.

Patterns

You can use these patterns as is or reduce or enlarge them to fit your needs. The Base Shapes are shown in red.

Meet Peggy Holt

I have been quilting since the revival of the craft in the early 1970s. My sewing career began at the age of nine with my first project in 4-H—the common gathered apron. Although I dabbled in the usual crafts of the seventies and eighties, quilting continued to become more and more important to me. Eventually, other avenues of creative expression fell by the wayside and I became a full-fledged quilter.

My personal quilt journey has taken me from the familiar block pattern quilts to being my own designer. Today my quilts are more likely to have innovative techniques and include intricate piecing or experimental techniques. I make quilts because they just have to come out of my head to let me sleep! Most of my work is in the art classification rather than the bed-covering classification. I love pushing the envelope, using unconventional materials such as metals, paints, plastics, and fibers.

I began my longarm custom quilting business in 1997 and am mostly self-taught. I have taught quilting classes of various kinds and enjoy presentations to local and regional guilds and other organizations. In 2003 I was privileged to speak to a group of teachers in the Czech Republic. I also enjoy being a quilt judge at area fairs and shows.

Photo by Vicki J. Horn

Over the years my quilts have received numerous awards including Best of Show. My quilts have been juried into International Quilt Festival, Houston, and International Quilt Festival, Chicago. I have also had quilts displayed at MQX and Innovations, as well as at various local and regional shows.

Previous publications include an article for *Quilting Arts* magazine and inclusion in *Beautifully Embellished Landscapes* by Joyce Becker (C & T Publishing, 2001) and Renae Haddadin's *Amazing Ways to Use Circles & Rays* (AQS, 2010).

My husband, Bill, and I live in a valley of the Rocky Mountains of western Montana, where I am active in guild, church, and community chorus activities. We have a son, Jason. He and his wife, Sierra, are the parents of our beautiful grandchildren, Zora Rose and Linden Rustle. I invite you to visit my website at www.quiltrelated.weebly.com.

More AQS Books

This is only a small selection of the books available from the American Quilter's Society. AQS books are known worldwide for timely topics, clear writing, beautiful color photos, and accurate illustrations and patterns. The following books are available from your local bookseller, quilt shop, or public library.

#8523

#8531

#8528

#8529

#8238

#8532

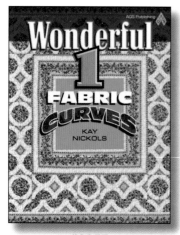

#8355

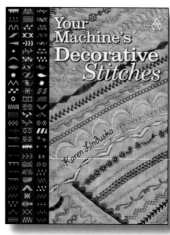

#8353

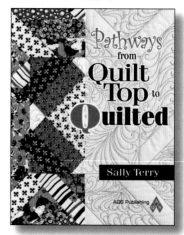

#8348

LOOK for these books nationally.
CALL or **VISIT** our website at

1-800-626-5420
www.AmericanQuilter.com